Great Ideas of the Renaissance

TRUDEE ROMANEK

Crabtree Publishing Company

www.crabtreebooks.com

Author: Trudee Romanek
Editor-in-Chief: Lionel Bender
Project coordinator: Kathy Middleton
Photo research: Susannah Jayes
Design concept: Robert MacGregor
Designer: Ben White
Production coordinator: Ken Wright
Production: Kim Richardson
Prepress technician: Ken Wright

Consultant: Lisa Mullins, Department of History and
    Philosophy of Science, University of Cambridge

Cover photo: Raphael (Raffaello Sanzio) (1483-1520)
    School of Athens, detail of left half showing Pythagoras
    (seated). Ca. 1510-1512. Fresco.
    Location :Stanza della Segnatura, Stanze di Raffaello,
    Vatican Palace, Vatican State
    Photo Credit : Scala / Art Resource, NY

Photographs and reproductions:
The Granger Collection, NYC/TopFoto: pages 4, 5, 6, 7, 9, 10,
    12, 13, 14, 17, 18, 21, 28, 29, 30, 31.
iStockphoto.com: pages 11, 19, 23, 25.
Topfoto: pages 1, 15, 27; A©RIA Novosti: page 20; Alinari
    Archives, Florence: pages 22, 24 (Reproduced with the
    permission of Ministero per i Beni e le Attivit Culturali),
    26; HIP/The Print Collector: page 8; Luisa Ricciarini:
    page 16.

Photo on page 1: Painting of Luca Pacioli, attributed to
    Jacopo de' Barbari, 1459. Pacioli is demonstrating a theo
    rem by Euclid.

This book was produced for Crabtree Publishing Company
    by Bender Richardson White

Library and Archives Canada Cataloguing in Publication
Romanek, Trudee
    Great ideas of the Renaissance / Trudee Romanek.
(Renaissance world) Includes index.
ISBN 978-0-7787-4596-9 (bound).--ISBN 978-0-7787-4616-4
(pbk.)

    1. Renaissance--Juvenile literature. 2. Europe--
Intellectual
life--Juvenile literature. 3. Europe--Civilization--Juvenile literature.
I. Title. II. Series: Renaissance world (St. Catharines, Ont.)

CB361.R64 2010   j940.2'1   C2009-902428-4

Library of Congress Cataloging-in-Publication Data
Romanek, Trudee.
    Great ideas of the Renaissance / Trudee Romanek.
    p. cm. -- (Renaissance world)
    Includes index.
    ISBN 978-0-7787-4616-4 (pbk. : alk. paper) -- ISBN 978-0-
7787-4596-9 (reinforced library binding : alk. paper)
    1. Renaissance--Juvenile literature. 2. Europe--Intellectual
life--Juvenile literature. 3. Europe--Civilization--Juvenile literature. I. Title. II. Series.

CB361.R645 2010   940.2'1--dc22

                                         2009016727

Crabtree Publishing Company

www.crabtreebooks.com   1-800-387-7650
Copyright © **2010 CRABTREE PUBLISHING COMPANY**. All rights reserved. No part of this publication may be reproduced,
stored in a retrieval system or be transmitted in any form or by any means, electronic, mechanical, photocopying, recording, or otherwise,
without the prior written permission of Crabtree Publishing Company. In Canada: We acknowledge the financial support of the Government
of Canada through the Book Publishing Industry Development Program (BPIDP) for our publishing activities.

Published in Canada
Crabtree Publishing
616 Welland Ave.
St. Catharines, Ontario
L2M 5V6

Published in the United States
Crabtree Publishing
PMB16A
350 Fifth Ave., Suite 3308
New York, NY 10118

Published in the United Kingdom
Crabtree Publishing
White Cross Mills
High Town, Lancaster
LA1 4XS

Published in Australia
Crabtree Publishing
386 Mt. Alexander Rd.
Ascot Vale (Melbourne)
VIC 3032

Contents

The Renaissance

The period in European history known as the Renaissance, meaning "rebirth," is famous for its explosion of new ideas. Many of these were ideas from past civilizations, revisited by great Renaissance thinkers and incorporated into their work in new ways.

Attitudes

During the Renaissance, which lasted from the early 1300s until the mid 1600s, people's attitudes changed dramatically. Views on religion, which had always dominated their lives and thinking, were starting to change. Scholars who studied ancient writings from Rome and Greece believed that they could become better people by learning. Instead of simply memorizing the old texts, scholars studied and questioned the information that those texts held.

A new interest in the human body led to detailed studies of **anatomy**. The quest for knowledge also led to the exploration of Earth, and the invention of new tools that could assist in examining objects near and far. To scholars of the time, the world was suddenly full of new places and ideas to explore, discover, and develop.

Renaissance inventor Leonardo da Vinci made sketches of dozens of new machines, including this device to let people breathe under water.

Paid to Think

Italy was the birthplace of many of the great artistic ideas of the Renaissance. This was due, in part, to a change in how artists were treated and paid. Through the 1300s, the **Catholic Church** was the major **patron** of artists. When it wanted a new work of religious art for a church or chapel, it paid an artist to create it.

In the 1400s, wealthy families, such as the Medici family in Italy, began to support artists themselves. They hired different painters, sculptors, and architects to create works of art and buildings for them. They paid for everything the artist would need while he worked, for however long it would take. This increase in available money gave artists more time and materials to experiment with new techniques, and to be creative and generate new ideas.

Spreading the Word

Up until the mid 1400s, books were produced by hand and copied in ink. Copying by hand was a specialist skill, and those who had trained to write in different styles were known as scribes. Books were expensive because of the materials used and the time it took to copy one book , so very few people owned them. Most books available were religious texts. In 1455, Johannes Gutenberg printed more than 100 copies of the Bible on his printing press, the first one in Europe. He went on to print many other books.

As printing became more common, it became cheaper to produce books. More people could afford to own them, and more of the new ideas of the Renaissance were published and shared throughout Europe and the world.

*This is a page of Gutenburg's printed Latin Bible. Artists often added artwork to printed books just as monks painted **illuminations** into manuscripts that they had copied by hand.*

TIMELINE

1348: the plague, or Black Death, arrives in Europe

1419: Brunelleschi designs the Orphans Hospital in Florence, the first example of Renaissance architecture

1455: Gütenberg Bible, the first printed book in Europe, is complete

1469: Leonardo da Vinci starts to train as a sculptor, painter, designer, and innovator

1492: Christopher Columbus lands in the Americas

1517: Martin Luther posts his 95 Theses on a church door in Germany, setting the Protestant Reformation in motion

1525: Soldiers in the battle of Pavia use recently invented handheld firearms

1534: Henry VIII declares himself head of the Church of England, breaking away from the Catholic Church

1543: Copernicus publishes his theory arguing that the Sun, rather than the Earth, is at the center of the universe

early 1590s: Shakespeare writes his first plays, Henry VI, parts 1, 2 and 3

Religion

By the early Renaissance, most of Europe followed the Roman Catholic Church and religion. Then people began to question its methods and practices, and world religion changed forever.

Corruption

By the early 1500s, the Catholic Church seemed to be focused on making money and holding power rather than saving souls. Priests sold "indulgences"—pieces of paper that forgave a sinner of his sins for a price. Church leaders appointed their relatives as influential **cardinals**. Others were bribed to give a cardinalship. Even within the Catholic Church, many people realized that a change of attitude was needed.

Two Critics

Desiderius Erasmus, a Catholic scholar, spent six years living in a Dutch monastery. What he saw there convinced him that the Church was not perfect. He wrote essays criticizing the wealthy and the religious, and theorizing on how education and religion could be improved. Historians believe his writings set the stage for change in religion.

Martin Luther was a German monk who was not impressed with how the Church was being run and the **corruption** among its leaders in Rome. In 1517, determined to improve the Catholic Church, he wrote the 95 Theses, a list of criticisms, and nailed it to a church door. It questioned the Church's practice of selling indulgences instead of urging people not to commit the sins in the first place. The list was printed and spread throughout Europe. Luther hoped it would encourage change within the Church. Instead, it inspired many to question whether they should continue following their beliefs.

This painting shows Pope Sixtus IV with the three nephews he appointed as cardinals, abusing his authority in a way that many other Renaissance popes did as well.

Change

As a result of Luther's criticisms, many people broke away from the Catholic Church in a movement known as the Protestant Reformation. They formed groups such as the Lutherans, led by Martin Luther, and the Calvinists in Switzerland who followed French lawyer Jean Calvin. Gradually, the anti-Catholic movement and attitude spread. Henry VIII, the King of England, declared in 1534 that the Church of England, or the Anglican Church, would no longer answer to the Pope in Rome but be a totally separate religion and Church.

As the control of the Catholic Church loosened, artists and thinkers had the chance to present images and thoughts the Church would not have encouraged or even allowed. It was an ideal time for the hatching of new and great ideas.

Persecution

The Catholic Church was not happy to lose so many members. In 1544 it formed the Roman Inquisition to put Protestant followers on trial for **heresy.** In spite of this, the Protestant faiths continued to gain followers. Wars broke out in the struggle for religious freedom. Protestants burned Catholics at the stake. Catholics slaughtered Protestant followers. Many lives were lost on both sides in European countries including France, Italy, Spain, England, and Germany, all in the name of religion.

Martin Luther listed his criticisms of the Catholic Church in a document called the 95 Theses. *Though his goal was to reform the Church, Luther's writings inspired a movement called Protestantism.*

People and Possibilities

Petrarch, an Italian scholar of the 1300s, was the first to recognize that during the **Middle Ages** human learning had taken a downward turn, away from the wisdom of the ancient people. With his ideas, he sparked a new movement known as humanism.

Humanism

When the first scholars of Europe studied the classical texts of the Roman and Greek civilizations, they interpreted them according to their own Christian view of the world. Renaissance scholars and **humanists** instead began to look at the texts on their own, and moved away from the earlier focus on Christianity.

Humanists celebrated the great things humans could do and had done in past civilizations, especially in literature and the arts. There was a growing awareness that a person could change his or her nature and place in society just by learning. However, men continued to hold the power. Women were considered inferior to men and did not have many rights or privileges, including access to most forms of training and education.

Dutch scholar Desiderius Erasmus is often called the "Prince of the Humanists." Erasmus strongly supported the humanist movement even while remaining a devout Catholic. He believed it was possible to strive for learning and encourage human abilities without losing sight of Christian goals. Through his travels, he helped to spread humanism throughout England.

*Erasmus and other humanists urged the study of the "human" arts—grammar, discussion, poetry, **ethics**, and history. He published books criticizing society and the Church, but also published translations of the Bible.*

Learning it All

Renaissance scholars valued the amount of learning each person was able to achieve. They believed that it was up to men, especially scholars and artists, to try to understand the world by studying it. They wanted to learn everything there was to know, an idea called universality.

Scholars studied Latin in order to read the classical texts. Some also studied Greek. They tried to understand as much of mathematics, science, and art as they could and worked to gain other skills such as singing, riding, and writing poetry. The more knowledge a man had, the more he was respected.

Renaissance Man

There were some men alive during the Renaissance period who managed to become accomplished in an amazing number of fields. History books now refer to them as "Renaissance men." Though Leonardo da Vinci was the most notable, there were many others. Italian Michelangelo became famous for his incredible sculptures, architectural designs, and paintings, but he also wrote poetry.

Leon Battista Alberti was another Italian architect, sculptor, and painter, but he also studied mathematics and science and was a poet, inventor, and archer. Galileo Galilei, also Italian, is remembered as a scientist, **philosopher**, and inventor of the telescope. He was also a good painter and lute player.

Leonardo

Leonardo da Vinci was the ultimate Renaissance Man. He was a brilliant Italian painter, sculptor, scientist, engineer, and inventor who knew a great deal about mathematics, botany, philosophy, geology, and architecture. Da Vinci was among the first to **dissect** human bodies, making drawings that greatly helped scientists understand anatomy. He also designed bridges and drew sketches of devices that have a lot in common with the modern helicopter, parachute, tank, and more.

Renaissance man Leonardo da Vinci created many works of art, including the famous Mona Lisa. *He sketched this red chalk self-portrait in about 1514, at the age of 62.*

Education

In the Middles Ages, most children who were educated were taught to memorize religious texts in Latin by monks and priests in a monastery or cathedral. The Renaissance brought the opportunity for children and adults to learn more than just religious writings, providing a broader education and a chance for a better job.

What to Study

The Protestant Reformation declared that people should be able to read sacred texts, previously all in Latin, in their own language. Students who did not read Latin or Greek could now study important books translated into their vernacular, or everyday language. This also meant people could understand what they were reading rather than just memorizing it.

The humanist movement also encouraged the study of many non-religious writings. Those manuscripts, carefully copied by the Church since classical times, began to be studied in schools.

Who Could Learn

For most of the Renaissance period there were two kinds of schooling: Private education by a tutor hired by the student's parents, or **communal** schools that were run by the city or town. Both of these cost a family money, so usually it was only the sons of the wealthy, **nobles**, or the successful merchants and craftsmen who got any education. Girls were rarely sent to school outside the home, regardless of their family's wealth. Since women were intended to marry and look after the children, it was not thought important for them to be educated.

Children lucky enough to go to school usually began their studies at age 6 or 7. Even young schoolchildren like these were expected to dress and behave like miniature adults.

Books

Probably the largest factor to change education during the Renaissance was the introduction of the printing press. Johannes Gutenberg's machine was modeled after other presses, which were tools used to squeeze juice from grapes and olives.

Gütenberg arranged his movable type—individual raised letters sticking up from blocks of metal—backwards in a holder to print the words in correct letter order on a page. He rolled ink over the type and then pressed a sheet of paper onto the inked letters to print the words. What made Gütenberg's invention so important was that it allowed him to print many copies of a page easily and quickly. He could re-ink and press the type to make many copies, before he changed the arrangement of letters and printed the next page.

Printing with movable type made it so much easier, faster, and cheaper to copy books that it was no longer just the wealthy who could afford them. Printing in this way also meant that books of any kind could be copied and sold, not just the religious texts copied by scribes. More books on a wide variety of subjects meant it was possible for more people to learn, become knowledgeable, and get a broad education.

England's Oxford University is the oldest university in the English-speaking world, founded some time during the 1100s. The university library contains many manuscripts and Renaissance printed books that are still used by scholars today.

Higher Learning

With the new emphasis on learning, many more wealthy Renaissance families wanted their sons to benefit from a good education. Rulers and city governments believed that education was important and so they created more places for scholars to learn. Between 1400 and 1625, the number of universities in Europe more than doubled, from 29 to over 70.

Medicine and Anatomy

The Renaissance quest for knowledge drove people to learn more about many things, including the human body. Early physicians and scientists made important breakthroughs that eventually allowed a better understanding of illnesses and their appropriate treatments.

Treating the Sick

Renaissance doctors believed that people's bodies were made up of a mixture of four different fluids they called "humors," one of which was blood. A physician's explanation and treatment for an illness usually involved increasing or decreasing whichever humor he thought was causing the problem.

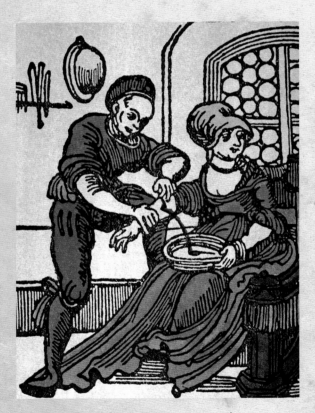

This woodcut shows a surgeon cutting a patient to let out the "bad" blood. Surgeons had to avoid cutting arteries or nerves or the patient could bleed to death or be partially paralyzed.

Barber-surgeons were men who performed minor medical treatments along with haircuts and shaves. If a barber-surgeon thought a patient had too much blood or "bad" blood, he would apply leeches to suck some of it from the patient. Surgeons, who were more skilled, might also perform a blood-letting, cutting into the patient to release the bad blood.

Disease

During the Renaissance the bubonic plague, a deadly infectious disease, swept through Europe and most of the world, killing millions of people. With so little medical knowledge, hospitals and their workers could not offer patients much helpful treatment, especially against the plague or influenza, another dangerous disease of that age. They did, however, try to keep the sick separate from the healthy and in that way prevented some spread of disease. During the 1400s, that idea of isolation led to a ban that prevented used-clothing sellers from dealing in clothes worn by people who had had leprosy. As a result that disease was nearly wiped out.

Anatomy and Dissection

Up until the early 1400s, dissecting human corpses to study their anatomy was not allowed. More than 1,000 years earlier a Greek physician named Galen had dissected monkeys and dogs, and had published his findings to help scientists understand the biology of humans. The only information Renaissance doctors had about the inside structure of the human body came from the centuries-old writings of Galen.

In the 1200s a few dissections of human corpses were allowed. The men doing the dissecting were expecting to find what Galen had written about. As a result, they did not trust the real details of human anatomy that they found. Hundreds of years later, Leonardo da Vinci was one of the first people to learn from dissecting human corpses. By 1510 he had drawn hundreds of accurate sketches based on some 30 dead bodies he dissected, though he did not publish those sketches.

About 30 years later another anatomist, Andreas Vesalius, published a book called *On the Fabric of the Human Body,* based on the repeated human dissections he had performed as a university anatomy instructor. This illustrated book described the reality of human anatomy.

The corpses that were dissected in university anatomy classes, like the one shown in this painting, were usually those of executed criminals. Leonardo da Vinci dissected hospital patients who had died.

Ambroise Paré

The good ideas of French battlefield surgeon Ambroise Paré improved patient treatments. Paré had been taught to pour boiling oil into a gunshot wound to treat it. One day, he ran out of oil and instead applied a mixture of egg yolks, turpentine, and rose oil. The next day, the patients who received that mixture were fairing better than the ones who had received the painful boiling oil treatment. Paré also developed better methods of **amputating** limbs.

Astronomy and Mathematics

Leading into the Renaissance, the fields of astronomy and mathematics were filled with theories that were centuries old. The spirit of learning and creativity of the age resulted in a new understanding of the universe and some important advances in mathematics.

The Universe

Ancient philosophers and star-gazers such as Pythagoras, Aristotle, and Ptolemy had stated that the Earth was the center of the universe and that the planets and Sun traveled in circles around it. The Church also supported this theory. Polish Renaissance astronomer Nicolas Copernicus believed there was a problem with Ptolemy's explanation of the universe. After observing the stars and using complicated mathematics, Copernicus concluded that if the planets were traveling in circles, they must be moving not around the Earth, but around the Sun.

Johann Kepler

In 1609, German astronomer Johann Kepler published a book explaining that the planets traveled not in circles but in oval paths. He also showed that the planets sped up or slowed down depending on where they were in these oval, or elliptical, orbits. Modern astronomers still use Kepler's laws of planetary motion. As well, questions about these orbits led scientists of his age and later to study a new topic—gravity, the pulling force of big objects.

In 1543, Copernicus published his explanation. Although the Church delcared it false, many agreed with his theory since it helped explain why days were longer at certain times of the year, something they could see for themselves.

This 1660 model of the universe, based on Copernicus's theory, shows the Sun circled by Mercury, Venus, Earth with its moon, Mars, Jupiter with its four moons, and Saturn. Neptune and Pluto were discovered much later.

Galileo

The study of astronomy received another enormous boost when Galileo Galilei built his own telescope, modeled on one in Holland that was being used to see distant objects across land and sea. Galileo aimed his telescope out into space and immediately realized that the universe contained many more stars and much more distant stars than anyone had ever suspected. He made many other observations, such as that the Moon's surface was not smooth as everyone thought.

Galileo was the first to observe the movement of the four largest moons of Jupiter. What he learned about their pattern of movement soon assisted sailors trying to navigate, or find their way, at sea.

Mathematics

During the Renaissance period, mathematicians in Europe started using some great ideas they had learned from Middle Eastern specialists. They began to switch from Roman numerals to the Hindu system of numbers still in use today. As well, they slowly started to use some of the Hindu-Arabic short-form methods of writing out problems. In the mid 1500s, Welshman Robert Recorde created the equals sign (=) and the plus (+) and minus (–) signs. In 1637 René Descartes, a French philospher, showed mathematicians how they could use equations to describe the size and shape of objects, rather than having to draw them.

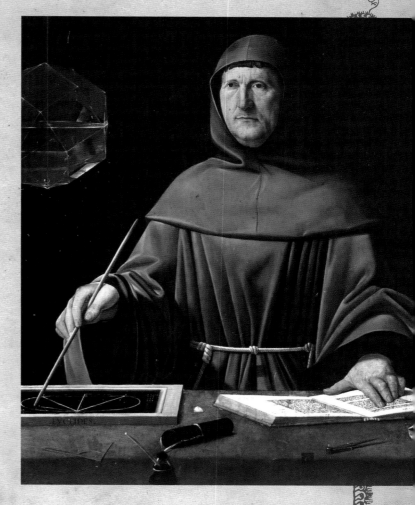

Renaissance mathematician Luca Pacioli was an important teacher of mathematics in northern Italy. He published books about geometry and proportion, a field of mathematics that greatly influenced Renaissance art.

Arithmetic was becoming more important to busy merchants who needed to keep better records. **Geometry** was becoming an essential tool for explorers trying to navigate and for artists striving to make their artwork more realistic. Soon these two fields of mathematics were being taught to more and more elementary students.

Renaissance artists began to paint scenes from mythology and real life, instead of just religious scenes commissioned by and for the Church. Their goal was to create realistic scenes. New techniques and experimentation led to new styles of artwork.

Math in Art

During the Renaissance the study of geometry helped artists use two new techniques—proportion and perspective—to make their paintings more realistic. Artists began to calculate how large to draw a person's head, for example, in relation to his height or the length of his arm. This was known as proportion. Italian Giotto di Bondone was one of the first to paint proportioned figures, in the early 1300s.

Artists also used geometry to add **perspective, scale,** and proportion to make their painted scenes look true to life. Previously, painters had often made people and objects in their paintings larger if they were important and smaller if they were not. Renaissance artists painted things in the front of the picture larger than those shown in the background or further away in the scene. They also used light and shadow to add depth. They would decide where the light was coming from in their scene and paint the objects near that light as brighter than those back in the shadows.

This painting uses perspective. The columns in the background are smaller than those in the **foreground,** *just as in real life columns that are further away would appear to be smaller.*

Michelangelo

Michelangelo Buonarroti is one of the most famous artists of the Renaissance. He is best known for his sculptures and frescoes. His most famous works of art include a marble sculpture of the biblical character *David* and the 40 frescoes of Old Testament scenes that cover the ceiling of the Vatican's Sistine Chapel, illustrating more than 300 characters. Michelangelo spent four years painting these frescoes.

Art Forms

Frescoes were very popular during the Renaissance. To create one, an artist would use water-based paint to paint a life-sized scene on a large wall or ceiling that was still wet with fresh plaster. The plaster and paint then dried together. A fresco artist had to work quickly to paint each new section of plaster before it dried.

In the early 1400s, Dutch artist Jan van Eyck was one of the first Renaissance painters to experiment with oil paints. These did not dry as quickly as paints made with water. That extra time gave artists the opportunity to make changes. The paints soon became popular with many artists.

Sculpture was another popular art form of the time. Artists were inspired by the sculptures of ancient Greece and Rome to create sculptures **cast** in bronze or carved from wood or stone. These were usually made to decorate a church or a tomb.

Masters

There were many great, innovative artists during the Renaissance. Leonardo da Vinci created a technique in which the wet oils at the edges of figures and background blurred to create *sfumato,* from the Italian word for smoke. Raphael was especially known for his religious paintings. The artist Titian helped to popularize portraits that showed the whole body, rather than just the head and shoulders. All three artists were Italian.

This detail is from 'The Last Judgment,' *a frescoe painted by Italian artist, Michelangelo, on a wall of the Sistine Chapel in the Vatican, Rome, more than 20 years after he completed his masterpiece on the chapel's ceiling.*

Literature and Drama

Huge changes in literature and an explosion of creativity were brought about by a shift away from writing only about religious themes, and in Latin. Poems and plays became extremely popular, and the novel, a completely new form of writing, was born.

Like most hand-copied manuscripts, this page from Dante's Divina Commedia *is decorated with hand-painted artwork. Printers often left space in early printed books so owners could pay artists to add decorations.*

Language

In the late Middle Ages, a few people began writing in common, everyday languages. Dante Alighieri wrote a long poem called *Divina Commedia* in Italian. This work was the first to deal with such serious matters as free will, faith, and salvation in everyday language. In England, Geoffrey Chaucer wrote *The Canterbury Tales* in his native tongue, making English writing popular.

Renaissance poet Petrarch wrote **epic** poems in Latin, but he also wrote 14-line poems called **sonnets** in the Italian dialect of Tuscan. His work inspired many later writers to write sonnets in their own languages. William Shakespeare wrote, in English, some of the most famous and admired sonnets of all time.

With inexpensive books available, thanks to the printing press, it became possible to write books for more than just the upper classes. Books in everyday languages telling stories not from the Bible became very popular among middle-class people, who usually could not read Latin.

New Forms

As writers experimented with sonnets, **odes** —lyrical, often musical verses—and other types of poetry, writing styles and stories changed. Luis Vas de Camões wrote a very successful poem about the history of Portugal, and Italian Ludovcio Ariosto's epic poem called *Orlando furioso* turned out to be a bestseller during the Renaissance.

Writers also began experimenting with prose, a type of writing that was not poetry but more like spoken language. In Italy, Boccaccio wrote that region's first prose work —a collection of tales called the *Decameron.* French writer François Rabelais wrote the first real novel, called *Gargantua and Pantagruel,* a story about the adventures of a man and his son. The highly popular novel *Don Quixote* was written in Spain by Miguel de Cervantes. Its success helped to establish the novel as a worthwhile literary form.

Drama

During the Renaissance plays became popular with both the upper and lower classes. The stories they presented had much in common with the lives people were living, rather than being the old-style religious dramas or **morality** plays about how to be a good person. In England plays written in everyday English became popular and the first permanent theaters were built. Soon, being a playwright or actor was considered an occupation not a hobby. Women were not allowed on stage, however.

Many late-Renaissance plays, including several written by Shakespeare, were staged at London's Globe Theatre, one of the first permanent theaters. This modern reconstruction of the Globe was built in 1997.

Playwrights

Some important Renaissance playwrights included Hans Sachs of Germany and Spain's Lope Felix de Vega Carpio. In England, Christopher Marlowe and Ben Jonson were very successful, though by far the most famous dramatist was William Shakespeare. Some of his most well-known plays include *King Lear, Hamlet, and Romeo and Juliet.* Shakespeare's characters were very different from earlier characters because they recognized flaws in their own personalities and struggled to change and improve themselves.

Music

Music blossomed in the Renaissance. New types of music and instruments were created, melody lines were combined, and the first great composers began creating. Like painters, musicians became recognized as respectable artists.

Voices

At this time Flemish musicians in the Netherlands began using a technique called imitation. One voice would begin singing and then another would enter a little later, repeating the melody, and then another would join and so on. This led to music in which different melodies are sung by different voices. For sacred or church music especially, whole choirs were divided into the four parts of soprano, alto, tenor, and bass, instead of all chanting one melody together as they had done in earlier times.

Some early Flemish composers, including Josquin Desprez and Adrian Willaert, traveled to Rome and other areas, sharing their new techniques with the rest of Europe. Giovanni Pierluigi da Palestrina, from Italy, is one of the most famous Renaissanace composers of sacred vocal music.

Instruments

In Venice, Italy, musicians developed the idea of different instruments playing different lines of music. This led to the creation of orchestras. The printing industry in Venice was thriving and so this new style of music could be easily printed and learned by individuals away from rehearsal.

The lute, a stringed instrument like a guitar, was a popular instrument all through the Renaissance. It was mostly used to play secular, or non-religious, music. Organs, already popular in the Middle Ages, were improved for better sound. By the 1500s early forms of most stringed, woodwind, and brass instruments were created, such as the guitar, trombone, and a keyboard called the harpsicord. Many of these were based on older instruments that had been brought to Europe from the Middle East.

Instruments such as the piano, oboe, trumpet, cello, and violin (shown here) were first developed in Europe during the Renaissance.

Musical Forms

Certain types of songs performed by singers, such as the French **chanson** and the **madrigal**, were very popular during the 1400s and 1500s. The lute was often the instrument played to accompany a madrigal.

The most important new form of music to develop out of the Renaissance was the opera. At first, performers recited the lyrics in a sort of chanted style called a **recitativo**. The singing of the words to various melodies developed from there. Opera encouraged the development of the orchestra as well, so that singers had instruments to accompany them.

Italian composer Claudio Monteverdi was the first great composer of operas. Opera houses were soon built across Europe because his operas were so successful. Unlike the theaters in England, these were like private clubs, and only the noble people could attend the performances.

The printing process meant sheets of music like this could be taken home for learning. This allowed for more complicated music, since the musicians did not have to memorize it. Notes were and still are written on a five-line "stave."

Birth of Ballet

In 1571 the performers who entertained Catherine de Medici, Queen of France, performed a dance in honor of a wedding. That dance, called *Ballet Comique de la Reine,* is thought to be the first ballet ever performed. It was accompanied by instrumental music as well as singing, and it was more than five hours long. More ballets followed in France, the birthplace of ballet.

Architecture

The great new ideas in Renaissance architecture, though very different from those of the Middle Ages that came before it, were not new at all. Many were based on even older designs from the Greek and Roman times.

Uncovering the Past

Up until this time the people of Rome had ignored the ancient ruins that thrust up out of the countryside, or they had taken the old stones to use in other buildings. During the Renaissance, the interest in the civilizations of more than 1,000 years before stirred an interest in ancient architecture.

In the late 1400s, Pope Sixtus IV decided that the streets of Rome should be widened. As workers dug the ground and prepared it for paving, they found some of the city's ancient ruins underneath. Then in 1527, more of these ruins were exposed when the oldest section of Rome was partially destroyed in battles.

Classical Ideas

Scholars interested in ancient times were able to study the now visible ruins and better understand ancient Roman ideas. They shared their findings with architects who became fascinated with the classical designs. During the 1500s the architects incorporated the elegant lines and decorations of those ancient structures into their own designs for churches, palaces, and bridges.

Constructing a large building costs a lot of money. For that reason, architecture changed more slowly than other aspects of Renaissance life. As time passed and the style became popular, architects and their customers took more risks and buildings included more classical elements.

In Venice, Michelozzo di Bartolommeo designed the Palazzo Medici with its many columns and rounded arches. Other architects also included such classical elements in their designs for private mansions.

A New Look

Starting in Florence and Rome, churches and other buildings with wide, rounded arches, columns, and strong horizontal lines gradually replaced buildings created in the gothic style, with their high vaulted ceilings and tall pointed arches. From these cities, the use of classical designs spread throughout Italy and beyond.

Famous Buildings

The earliest example of Renaissance architecture, according to historians, was Florence's Ospedale deglie Innocenti, a hospital for orphans. Filippo Brunelleschi designed it based on mathematical symmetry—each arch in the hospital's long colonnade was the same distance across as it was high, and depth of the space behind each was that same distance.

Brunelleschi is also well-known for having designed the 130 foot (39.4 meter) wide orange dome that sits atop the cathedral in Florence. It was, at that time, the largest dome ever built and it required some ingenious architecture.

Andrea Palladio designed many impressive mansions outside Italy's cities. The style of these villas became known as "Palladian" and was recreated later in many English countryside homes as well as in plantations of the southern United States.

St. Peter's Basilica, an important church for the Pope in Italy, was considered the grandest building of the 1500s. Many architects, including, Bramante, Raphael, and Michelangelo, worked on its design.

The Architect

In the 1400s, many buildings were designed by artists and then built by masons, men skilled in the work of building with stone and brick. These builders would often make the decisions on how the structure would be created. By the early 1500s, many building designs were based on precise mathematics. Often a single person, the architect, created the designs, working closely with a patron. The architect also supervised the construction to make sure the plans were followed exactly.

Society and Power

The Renaissance brought a shift in power. People from the lower-class saw a chance to improve their lives by getting out from under the control of the upper classes. The old system of lord controlling peasants began to come apart.

Changing Times

In the Middle Ages, most people lived in a society in which dukes or kings and the nobility controlled the land, sometimes using violence to keep the **peasants** down in the lower class. The cities that existed were small and were home to nobility, merchants, and poor workers.

During the Renaissance, the merchants in cities increased their trading with other regions. In Italy, merchants became wealthy from trading with people in regions to the east of Europe. More people moved to the cities to take up the available work, and those cities grew. In Italy, cities such as Siena, Venice, and Florence, formed their own governments.

Kings, nobles, and other rulers fought over control of the cities and the land around them. Often two or more regions formed an alliance, and marriages between ruling families helped to cement these.

The marriage of Catherine de Medici, of the ruling family of Florence, to Henry II, son of the king of France, helped to form an alliance between the two regions.

Middle Class

Unlike the lower-class peasants, the growing middle class of merchants had money to spend on luxuries. Their desire for nicer homes, more education, and better food and clothing generated more business and helped the cities to grow wealthier. The middle class also purchased artwork, supporting the growing Renaissance art industry. The ruling class could not ignore this new, influential social group.

Rulers

In areas of Europe such as France and England, an individual person acted as the ruler. In others a council made group decisions. The city of Venice had a Grand Council and an elected senate as well as a leader called the doge who was chosen by the Council. This shift away from one person acting as ruler was a new concept during the Renaissance.

Many humanists and people in powerful positions debated what it meant to be a good ruler. They studied the classical texts of Greece and Rome to get tips on how to govern well. Niccolo Machiavelli wrote a famous book called *Il Principio*, or The Prince, that suggested the best way to rule was to be ruthless and dishonest.

Moving Up

If a man was a peasant farming the land of a lord, it was unlikely that he or his children would ever be anything but peasants. If he learned a trade or worked for a merchant, however, there was a much better chance that his family's life would improve.

If he, his wife, and children moved to a city, there were many more potential customers and chances of training and education.

An increasing number of peasants moved to the cities, looking for opportunities to be more in control of their own lives. A new class of people emerged, a middle-class of successful merchants and bankers. It sat between the poor lower class and the rich and royal upper class.

The town hall in Siena, Italy, was originally built as a home for the government that ran that city. It has stood in the main square of Siena since 1297.

Commerce

From about 1450, governments forged new trade routes between countries. More trade routes meant increased trading, which resulted in greater wealth for everyone. Those factors as well as changing attitudes caused an enormous increase in industry and business.

Trade Routes

The land we now call Italy was in the perfect place for trading during the Renaissance. To the east were the exotic regions of India and Asia. To the west, the rest of Europe waited, eager to buy valuable spices and other eastern products. Italy was surrounded by water, making it easy for traders to come and go.

The waterways of Italy provided better routes for transporting the eastern goods out toward the rest of Europe.

Other countries, especially Spain and Portugal, were eager to find other routes to these valuable goods. The rulers of both countries hired explorers to find a way to India and Asia by sea. In 1499, Vasco de Gama returned from navigating a route between Portugal and India. It was the search for trade routes to India that prompted Queen Isabella of Spain to send Christopher Columbus west, where he discovered North America. Later explorers brought back riches from South America.

The Catholic Church preached that lending money and charging interest was a sin. This picture shows the punishments people who made a profit from lending money could expect in Hell.

Business

During the Renaissance, banking was on the rise, in spite of the fact that the Catholic Church disapproved of people making money from charging interest. Families such as the Medicis in Florence, and later the Fuggers and Welsers in Germany, were growing and expanding, opening branches in other regions. Banks provided funds to finance new enterprises and voyages for trade. Owners of those banks earned money that they in turn spent on other products.

The printing industry, which was very busy in the 1500s, helped the economy grow. It also provided the means for other people to learn basic mathematics, new bookkeeping methods, and improvements in farming.

Tools of Commerce

New ideas in banking and commerce were developed during the Renaissance. Those who kept track of business dealings began to use double-entry bookkeeping. This was a much more accurate way of recording **transactions** and charting how much money was spent and how much was made.

In 1550, mass-produced coins, all the same size and weight, began to replace the irregular hand-made coins. All money during this period was in the form of coins. Carrying large amounts of money meant bringing a chest of coins along. An easier way to do business was to use bills of exchange instead.

Secret banking journals of the Medici family, whose portraits appear on the medallions. The small gold coins from Florence, called florins, were the most important currency in all of Renaissance Europe.

A bill of exchange was a written promise to pay money to someone, sometimes in another kind of coin, and at another bank. These written promises were similar to modern banknotes and checks.

Guilds

Craftsmen, bankers, stonemasons, and other workers belonged to groups called guilds. Each guild set prices, decided how much training its workers required, and made other decisions related to its particular trade. As a guild member, a young man had to first work as an apprentice, doing the least important tasks. He then traveled and worked as a **journeyman** before he could become a master and open a workshop.

Warfare

Renaissance fighters were already using gunpowder from China to fire their cannons. Further innovations brought new weapons, which meant defenses needed to change to keep up.

New Weapons

Religious differences and struggles over territory kept wars brewing throughout most of the Renaissance. Gunpowder had arrived in Europe from Asia during the Middle Ages. Now European countries began to produce it, bringing down its cost. Cheaper gunpowder made cannons and firearms much more attractive to warring armies, and these fired weapons become more popular.

Early firearms were not accurate and could not project objects long distances. Often, they were used alongside men fighting with swords and other weapons of the Middle Ages. Improvements in metal strength and firearm design resulted in better firearms later in the Renaissance.

Cannons, used in Europe since the 1200s, were improved. The lighter, more powerful weapons could be mounted on ship decks, along castle battlements, or mounted on wheels and dragged onto the battlefield.

Soldiers

Better weapons meant more fighters were injured, and so larger numbers of fighters were needed. These additional soldiers also needed to be better trained to succeed against the new weapons. Governments waging wars turned to professional fighters. Most soldiers during the Renaissance were mercenaries—professional soldiers hired and paid by a government to battle against its enemies on home territory or far away. These mercenaries usually had no personal ties to the region or master they fought for, though many fought to the death.

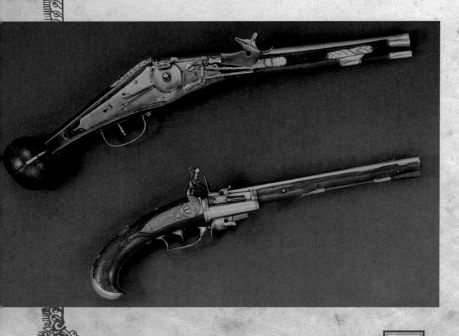

By the late 1500s, hand-held firearms such as this pistol (top) had been developed from larger guns and muskets. It was perfect for close fighting. A pistol of the 1800s (bottom) differed only in the firing mechanism.

Contract Killers

The Condottieri were a well-known group of mercenary leaders who were like generals. They were hired under a contract to provide a certain number of soldiers for a particular battle or time period. These leaders and their men were among the most respected soldiers of the Renaissance. Most of the Condottieri were from the Italian **city-states**, though a few, including England's Sir John de Hawkwood, were not.

Defenses

As weapons changed, so did defenses against them. Plates of steel armor were invented during the 1300s and by 1420 some soldiers were wearing full suits of body armor. These were made of separate plates that met at the joints so the fighter could bend. The steel was hard, though, and a shot fired against it could split the plate or shatter it, sending shards of dangerous metal into the flesh of the fighter.

The solution was to make the steel stronger, which made it heavier, and so it was only used to protect the head and vital organs. By 1600, soldiers were wearing heavy breast plates and plates of armor on their backs.

Castles no longer provided enough protection either. The new, stronger weapons could break through high castle walls too easily. During the 1500s new fortresses were built with low walls strengthened by built-up earth in behind them and topped with cannons.

Charles V, Holy Roman Emperor and King of Spain, spent much of his reign battling France and the Turks, as well as subduing revolts among the Spanish citizens and the Protestants.

Da Vinci's Weapons

Leonardo da Vinci, famous painter and sculptor, also engineered military weapons. His notebooks contain designs for many weapons, including a mounted gun with 10 barrels that could shoot a spray of shots over a wide area against oncoming troops. No one else in the Renaissance designed anything like these and, in fact, da Vinci's designs were not built in his lifetime either.

Everyday Life

Exploration, changing attitudes, new inventions, and new techniques developed during the Renaissance had a tremendous impact on the everyday lives of all people, from the poorest to the most noble.

Time

During the 1300s, large clocks in town squares were introduced that struck chimes on the hours. Some struck the hours one to 24 starting from sunset, others starting from sunrise. Still others struck one to 12 starting from midnight and noon, as modern clocks do. Very few of the early Renaissance clocks had minute hands.

Once clocks kept track of the hours, the workday could be measured and people could make appointments and schedule meetings. When portable clocks and pocket watches were invented during the 1500s, people no longer had to rely on hearing the chimes to know the time.

Meals

At meals during the Middle Ages, people at the table had all reached for their food from a shared platter. By the mid 1500s, they ate from individual plates. Gradually, Europeans ate with forks, instead of just knives and their fingers as in earlier times.

The food was plain. Only rich merchants, nobles, and royalty could afford the exotic spices arriving from Asia. Some foods, such as tomatoes, potatoes, most kinds of beans, and chocolate were not available until the 1600s, after they were brought over from America.

In northern Europe, people drank beer they had brewed. In the south they drank local wine. Both of these drinks were safer to drink than the water, which was often contaminated and could cause serious illness.

Smaller clocks, like this one made in 1589, could be kept at home, allowing people to keep better track of the hours as they passed.

Farming

Before the Renaissance grain farmers had always left their fields fallow, or at rest, for a season so as not to deplete the goodness from the soil. Now, they began using the fields for every season but adding animal manure to fertilize and replenish them. Instead of plowing parallel rows in the field and planting the seeds in those rows, farmers plowed another set of parallel rows across them. This cross plowing left more places for the seeds to take root and grow.

Clothing

The upper classes in the Renaissance wore bright garments of fine wool and linen or sometimes silk and velvet, whose pieces were tied together with laces or ribbons by their servants. The middle classes tried to copy the upper-class clothes. The lower classes wore clothing of coarse linen or wool in their natural colors since dye was expensive. Women wore long skirts and **bodices**. Men wore buttoned jackets and knee-length pants.

Most people began wearing underwear by the 1400s. Upper-class women were also wearing corsets, undergarments that went from the hips to just below the shoulders and could be tightened to change a woman's figure.

Not just in clothing, but in science, the arts, architecture, and society, many of the great ideas of the time have shaped modern life.

New farming techniques introduced in the Renaissance resulted in more crops. This painting shows farmers in about 1515 mowing wheat and tying it into sheaves to dry.

Sumptuary Laws

During the Renaissance sumptuary laws prohibited people from showing more wealth than suited their social class. These laws were strictly enforced so that people could tell the rich from the poor. It was illegal, for instance, for anyone except royalty to wear **ermine** fur. The lower classes could only wear lower-value furs such as fox or rabbit.

Further Reading and Web Sites

Hinds, Kathryn. *The City (Life in the Renaissance series).* New York: Benchmark, 2003. Also, *The Church, The Countryside and The Court.*

Quigley, Mary. *The Renaissance.* Heinemann, 2003.

Cole, Alison. *Eyewitness: Renaissance.* Dorling Kindersley, 2000.

Mason, Antony. *Everyday Life in Renaissance Times.* Minnesota: Smart Apple Media, 2005.

Schomp, Virginia. *The Italian Renaissance.* New York: Marshall Cavendish, 2003.

Exploring Leonardo: www.mos.org/sln/Leonardo/LeoHomePage.html

Renaissance: www.learner.org/interactives/renaissance/

The Renaissance: www.mrdowling.com/704renaissance.html

Glossary

amputate Cut off surgically

anatomy Study of the parts of the body

bodice Woman's garment covering from waist to shoulders

cardinal High official in the Catholic Church

cast To pour a liquid into a shaped mold to make an object

Catholic Church World's largest Christian church

chanson A music-hall song

city-state Region dominated by a city

communal Shared by everyone in a town

corruption Actions that are dishonest or abuse power

dissect Cut something up to study it

epic Long story about someone heroic

ermine white-furred weasel

ethics Sense of right and wrong

foreground Part of a scene nearest the front

geometry Mathematics of points, lines, surfaces and shapes

heresy Crime of disagreeing with the Church, often punishable by death

humanist Student of subjects that deal with human thought

illuminations Colorful manuscript decorations

journeyman One who travels for work experience

madrigal A song for two or three voices

Middle Ages Period before the Renaissance, from about 850 to 1350

morality A play presenting a lesson of right and wrong

nobles People of high social rank

ode Songlike poem showing the poet's feelings

patron Wealthy supporter of an artist

peasant Lower-class worker

perspective Drawing on a flat surface to create the look of depth

philosopher One who searches for wisdom

scale Size

sonnet A 14-line, rhymed poem

transaction Exchange of goods, services, or money

Index

Printed in China — CT